EXPLORE BIOMES

# TUNDRA BIOMES

BY CLARA MacCARALD

Kids Core
An Imprint of Abdo Publishing
abdobooks.com

abdobooks.com

Published by Abdo Publishing, a division of ABDO, PO Box 398166, Minneapolis, Minnesota 55439. 

Printed in the United States of America, North Mankato, Minnesota
052023
092023

THIS BOOK CONTAINS RECYCLED MATERIALS

Cover Photo: Shutterstock Images
Interior Photos: Josef Pittner/Shutterstock Images, 4–5; Michele Aldeghi/Shutterstock Images, 6; Gregory A. Pozhvanov/Shutterstock Images, 8; Frank Olsen, Norway/Moment/Getty Images, 10–11; Rebecca L. Latson/Moment/Getty Images, 13; Shawn Harrison/USGS Pacific Coastal and Marine Science Center/US Geological Survey/Science Source, 14; Shutterstock Images, 16, 18–19, 25, 28 (ox, fox), 29 (caribou, polar bear); Vita Serendipity/Shutterstock Images, 20; Alexandra Giese/Shutterstock Images, 22; Dennis W Donohue/Shutterstock Images, 26; Annstas Ag/Shutterstock Images, 28–29

Editor: Angela Lim
Series Designer: Ryan Gale

Library of Congress Control Number: 2022949105

Publisher's Cataloging-in-Publication Data

Names: MacCarald, Clara, author.
Title: Tundra Biomes / by Clara MacCarald
Description: Minneapolis, Minnesota: Abdo Publishing Company, 2024 | Series: Explore biomes | Includes online resources and index.
Identifiers: ISBN 9781098291143 (lib. bdg.) | ISBN 9781098277321 (ebook)
Subjects: LCSH: Tundras--Juvenile literature. | Biotic communities--Juvenile literature. | Habitats--Juvenile literature. | Life zones--Juvenile literature. | Tundra animals--Juvenile literature. | Tundra plants--Juvenile literature. | Tundra ecology--Juvenile literature.
Classification: DDC 577--dc23

# CONTENTS

Arctic wolves can weigh up to 155 pounds (70 kg).

CHAPTER 1

# A TUNDRA HUNT

A line of Arctic wolves runs across the tundra. A cold wind whips through their white fur. The hungry **predators** are searching for food. Their paws tread on rocks, mosses, and lichens. Rolling hills with few trees lie in the distance.

Despite their large size, musk oxen can reach speeds of 37 miles per hour (60 km/h).

It is the middle of the day. But the sun hangs low in the sky. The Arctic tundra does not get much sunlight in the fall. Soon the tundra will become even colder and darker. For four months of the year, the wolves will not see the sun at all.

The scent of musk oxen catches the wolves' attention. The wolves trot up a hill and see the herd. The huge, shaggy musk oxen feed on plants. Two of the musk oxen are calves. Young animals are easier for the wolves to kill.

### Lichens

Lichens are made of fungi and either algae or bacteria. The fungi take in water for the lichen. Algae and bacteria make food that it can use. There are approximately 15,000 types of lichens in the world. Some look crusty. Others are leafy and look like plants.

Plants on the Arctic tundra must be able to withstand cold temperatures.

The wolves move closer. But the musk oxen see them approach. The herd members huddle close together. The adults form a circle around the calves. They face the predators with their deadly horns. The oxen have strong hooves. They could badly hurt the wolves.

The wolves give up. The pack sniffs the air and moves on. The predators will need to find other **prey** to satisfy their hunger.

## Tundra Biomes

A biome includes the animals, plants, and nonliving things in a particular region. It also includes climate. Wolves and musk oxen are some of the animals that live on the tundra. The tundra has short plants such as mosses. Water is a nonliving part of the biome.

Tundra biomes are very cold. They have few trees. About 10 percent of Earth's surface is tundra.

### Explore Online

Visit the website below. Does it give any new information about musk oxen that wasn't in Chapter One?

### Musk Ox Fact Sheet

abdocorelibrary.com/tundra-biomes

The northern lights can often be seen in northern Norway and in the Arctic tundra close to the North Pole.

CHAPTER 2

# ALL ABOUT TUNDRA BIOMES

Soil on the tundra is frozen for most of the year. Most **precipitation** falls as snow. Summers on the tundra are short and cool. But summer temperatures are warm enough to melt some ice and snow.

There are two main kinds of tundra. The Arctic tundra circles the North Pole. It covers the northern parts of North America, Europe, and Asia. Some parts of Antarctica have biomes that are similar to the Arctic tundra. Alpine tundra regions are found above the tree line in mountains. The tree line is the highest place where trees grow.

## Arctic Tundra

The Arctic tundra receives less than 10 inches (25 cm) of precipitation each year. This biome can be considered a kind of desert. Temperatures are often below freezing for six to ten months of the year.

Alpine tundra can be found at elevations above 7,000 feet (2,130 m) in Mount Rainier National Park in Washington.

Climate change causes permafrost in the Arctic tundra to melt. This leads to soil washing away.

Melting snow provides moisture to the soil. It can form ponds and lakes during the summer. But some soil in the Arctic is frozen year-round. This frozen ground is called permafrost.

## Alpine Tundra

Alpine tundra can be anywhere in the world. This biome can even be found in warm parts of Earth. The harsh conditions high in the mountains make it difficult for people to live there, though some do. People may also visit alpine tundra for activities such as hiking and skiing.

### Ancient Permafrost

Scientists have found Arctic permafrost that has been frozen for at least 650,000 years. Permafrost can preserve ancient animals. The cold temperatures stop their bodies from breaking down. Many of the animals found in permafrost are mammoths. Finds also include a wolf pup, a caribou calf, and a lion cub from tens of thousands of years ago.

The Tibetan Plateau in Asia has alpine tundra at elevations above 11,480 feet (3,500 m).

Alpine tundra may have patches of permafrost. The precipitation in alpine tundra varies. Areas of alpine tundra in the Rocky Mountains may receive 25 inches (64 cm) of precipitation a year. But some alpine tundra biomes are very dry. The Himalayas are a mountain range in Asia. The alpine tundra there may receive less than 3 inches (7.6 cm) of precipitation each year.

## Further Evidence

Look at the website below. Does it give any new evidence to support Chapter Two?

### Tundra

abdocorelibrary.com/tundra-biomes

Caribou migrate south during the winter to avoid the coldest Arctic temperatures.

CHAPTER 3

# LIFE ON THE TUNDRA

Conditions on the tundra are harsh. The weather is cold for most of the year. The Arctic tundra also receives little sunlight in the fall and winter. Days are extremely short. The sun may not rise at all.

Reindeer lichen are food for large grazing animals in the Arctic, including caribou and musk oxen.

Cold temperatures and short days make it difficult for living things to survive. Living things on the tundra need special **adaptations** to survive.

## The Tundra throughout the Year

Plants on the Arctic tundra get enough sunlight and warmth to grow only six to ten weeks of the year. Plants burst into life when the snow melts. Insect populations grow.

Many birds, including snow geese, **migrate** to the tundra when it is warm. They eat and breed there. These animals fly away after the growing season is finished. Caribou herds on the Arctic tundra move south during winter. Mountain goats in alpine tundra move lower on the mountains.

Some animals **hibernate** to avoid the winter. Arctic ground squirrels sleep in burrows. They stay underground for about eight months. Grizzly bears use dens. They hibernate from fall to spring. Hibernating animals save energy. They do not need as much energy to move around or stay warm.

Marmots live in alpine tundra. They gather grasses to line their burrows, where they hibernate.

# Adaptations for the Cold

Insect and plant populations grow when the tundra warms. But temperatures can drop quickly, even in the summer. Tundra insects such as mosquitoes have a special chemical in their blood. This chemical keeps their blood from freezing. The creeping Arctic willow has leaves with fuzz that traps heat.

## Supercooled Squirrels

The body temperature of Arctic ground squirrels often falls below freezing while hibernating. No other hibernating animal gets as cold. But the squirrels' blood remains liquid. It does not freeze. This process is known as supercooling.

Tundra animals must be able to stay warm in the winter. Many grow warm feathers or thick coats of fur. Polar bears have white coats. The color blends in with snow and ice. Other adaptations include an Arctic fox's short ears. Because their ears are small, they do not lose heat as quickly as animals with larger ears.

## Humans and the Tundra

People drill for oil in the Arctic tundra. This can cause pollution that harms wildlife. But the biggest threat to the tundra is **climate change**. The Arctic is warming faster than other parts of the world.

# Arctic Fox Adaptions

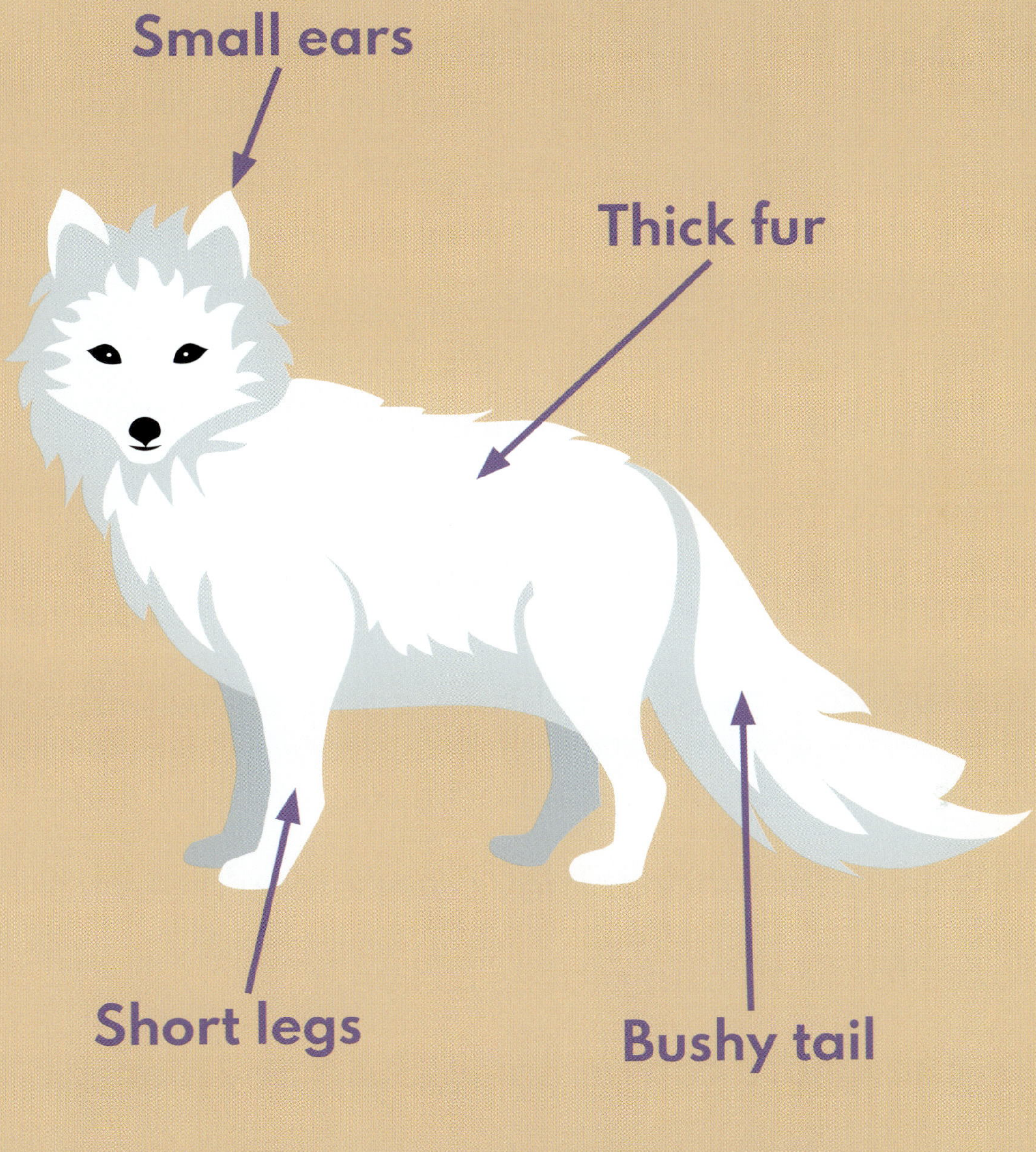


Arctic foxes have many adaptations that help them stay warm. Small body parts reduce heat loss.

Climate change affects animals that live in alpine tundra, such as snow leopards.

Warmer temperatures can cause many changes. Trees can grow in the warmer temperature. Forests are beginning to take over the tundra. Trees and shrubs compete with the lichen that caribou eat. Red foxes can survive in a warmer tundra. They compete with Arctic foxes for food and places to live.

The tundra can be harsh. But many plants and animals make their home in this biome. The tundra is changing. As it changes, it affects life on the tundra and around the world.

# PRIMARY SOURCE

Kimberley Miner is a scientist. She studies permafrost loss and other changes in the Arctic tundra. She says:

> Everyone is racing as fast as they can to understand what's going on at the poles. The more we understand, the better prepared we will be for the future.

Source: "Thawing Permafrost Could Leach Microbes, Chemicals into Environment." *NASA*, 9 Mar. 2022, climate.nasa.gov. Accessed 2 Dec. 2022.

## Point of View

What is the author's point of view on the Arctic tundra? What is your point of view? Write a short essay about how they are similar and different.

# EXPLORE THE BIOME

Many plants and animals help make up tundra biomes. Can you identify which parts of this tundra biome are plants? Which are animals? Can you find any nonliving parts of the biome?

# Glossary

**adaptations**
changes to a physical trait or behavior over a long period of time that allow a plant or animal to survive more easily in its biome

**climate change**
a long-term shift in weather patterns, such as rising temperatures

**hibernate**
to be inactive during the winter

**migrate**
to move from one area to another at a certain time of year, typically to find food or to breed

**precipitation**
liquid or frozen water that falls from the sky, including rain, sleet, and snow

**predators**
animals that hunt other animals for food

**prey**
an animal hunted by other animals for food

# Online Resources

To learn more about tundra biomes, visit our free resource websites below.

Core Library CONNECTION
FREE! COMMON CORE MULTIMEDIA RESOURCES

Visit **abdocorelibrary.com** or scan this QR code for free Common Core resources for teachers and students, including vetted activities, multimedia, and booklinks, for deeper subject comprehension.

Booklinks NONFICTION NETWORK
FREE! ONLINE NONFICTION RESOURCES

Visit **abdobooklinks.com** or scan this QR code for free additional online weblinks for further learning. These links are routinely monitored and updated to provide the most current information available.

# Learn More


Alkire, Jessie. *Arctic Foxes.* Abdo, 2019.

Ganeri, Anita. *Arctic and Antarctic.* DK, 2022.

Stine, Megan. *Where Is the North Pole?* Penguin Workshop, 2022.

# Index



# About the Author

Clara MacCarald is a freelance writer with a master's degree in ecology and natural resources. She lives with her family in an off-grid house nestled in the forests of central New York. When not parenting her daughter, she spends her time writing nonfiction books for kids.